WALL TO WALL

Mural Art around the World

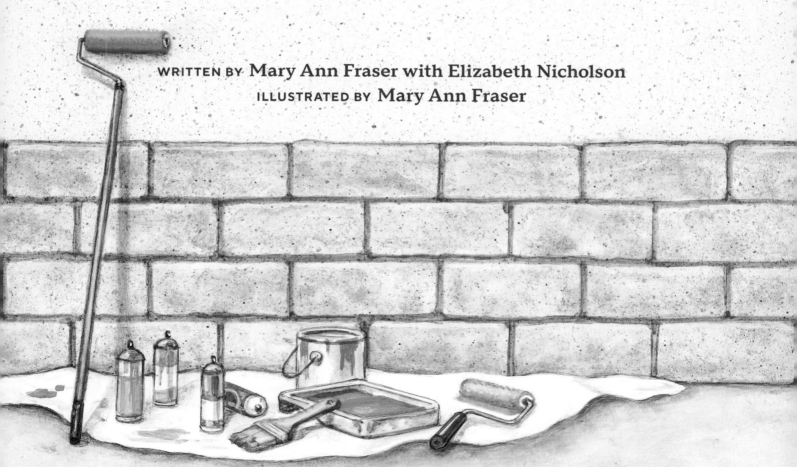

WRITTEN BY Mary Ann Fraser with Elizabeth Nicholson

ILLUSTRATED BY Mary Ann Fraser

Getty Publications, Los Angeles

UNITED STATES

UNITED STATES

MEXICO

ARGENTINA

Contents

1 INTRODUCTION

3 HANDS UP FOR ART
Cave of the Hands, Argentina

7 DIRECTIONS TO THE AFTERWORLD
Queen Nefertari's Tomb, Egypt

10 GIRL POWER
Mithila Kohbar, India

14 OUT OF THE ASHES
Herculaneum, Italy

19 ALONG THE SILK ROAD
Mogao Grottoes, China

22 GHOULS AND PRINCES
Qusayr 'Amra, Jordan

26 PICTURING THE MIDDLE AGES
Runkelstein Castle, Italy

28 SCULPTED IN PAINT
Sistine Chapel, Vatican City

32 HISTORY IN RELIEF
Palace Art of Abomey, Republic of Benin

36 ART REVOLUTION
The History of Mexico, Mexico

NORWAY

GERMANY

- - - - - - - - ITALY

VATICAN CITY

JORDAN

AFGHANISTAN

CHINA

REPUBLIC OF
BENIN

EGYPT

INDIA

40 **A NEW DEAL FOR PUBLIC ART**
Coit Tower Murals,
United States

43 **JUSTICE AND REMEMBRANCE**
Amistad Murals, United States

47 **TATTOO FOR A RIVER**
The Great Wall of Los Angeles,
United States

50 **ARRESTING ART**
Crack Is Wack, United States

55 **WALL OF WAR AND PEACE**
Berlin Wall, Germany

58 **FOR THE BIRDS**
Lilith and Olaf, Norway

62 **WHEN WORDS ARE NOT
ENOUGH**
Dreaming Graffiti, Afghanistan

66 **PRESERVING THE WORLD'S
MURALS**

68 **AFTERWORD: WHAT'S NEXT?**

68 **SELECTED SOURCES**

69 **ACKNOWLEDGMENTS**

70 **GLOSSARY**

71 **INDEX**

▲

Macro Mural of Palmitas by the Germen Crew, Pachuca, Mexico, 2015

The Germen Crew, a youth group known for graffiti and street art, turned 209 homes in the Palmitas neighborhood into one large, rainbow-colored mural.

◀

Gymnast by Banksy, Borodyanka, Ukraine, 2022

The famously anonymous street artist Banksy left this image on the wall of a building damaged during Russia's invasion of Ukraine.

Introduction

Walls are like big, blank canvases: they practically beg for someone to draw on them. Maybe you've colored on a wall—hopefully with permission. If you have, you are in good company. People have been drawing and painting on walls since prehistoric times. They draw to say "I was here." They draw to tell a story or express an idea. They draw about what they value and to record important events in their lives. And sometimes they draw simply to create beauty.

▲

Section of *Ethnicities* by Eduardo Kobra, Rio de Janeiro, Brazil, 2016

A giant mural in Brazil features Indigenous people from five continents, including this Mursi woman of Ethiopia.

Artwork painted on a wall, ceiling, or other permanent surface is called a mural. There are as many ways of making murals as there are colors in a paint box. Spray cans, hog bristles, flour paste, gold foil, rollers, eggs, twigs, cow urine—all of these and more have been used to decorate walls. Muralists have worked for pharaohs, popes, and kings; they have organized themselves into guilds, crews, and clubs. Their art adorns the interiors and exteriors of caves, tombs, temples, churches, palaces, private homes, and public buildings.

Murals are powerful tools; their size alone commands attention. They can preserve our shared history, honor our heroes, spark an uprising, demand change. They can replace neglect with color to transform a neighborhood. No matter the method, motive, or location, each picture painted onto a wall shows us where we've been and where we've yet to go.

Let's take a look!

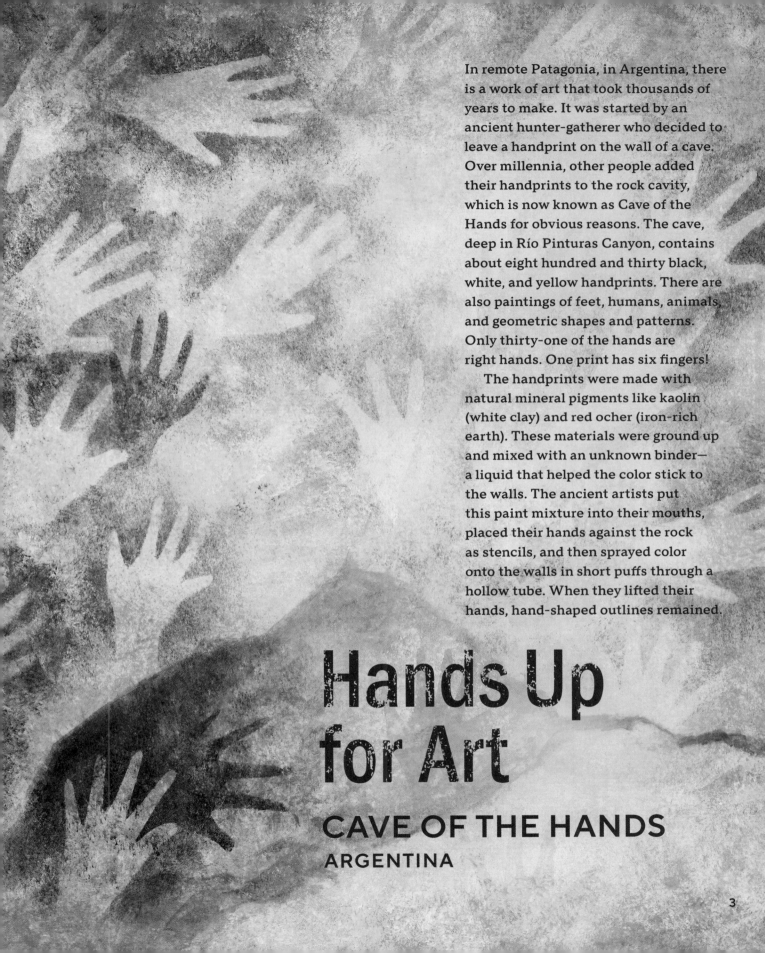

In remote Patagonia, in Argentina, there is a work of art that took thousands of years to make. It was started by an ancient hunter-gatherer who decided to leave a handprint on the wall of a cave. Over millennia, other people added their handprints to the rock cavity, which is now known as Cave of the Hands for obvious reasons. The cave, deep in Río Pinturas Canyon, contains about eight hundred and thirty black, white, and yellow handprints. There are also paintings of feet, humans, animals, and geometric shapes and patterns. Only thirty-one of the hands are right hands. One print has six fingers!

The handprints were made with natural mineral pigments like kaolin (white clay) and red ocher (iron-rich earth). These materials were ground up and mixed with an unknown binder— a liquid that helped the color stick to the walls. The ancient artists put this paint mixture into their mouths, placed their hands against the rock as stencils, and then sprayed color onto the walls in short puffs through a hollow tube. When they lifted their hands, hand-shaped outlines remained.

Hands Up for Art

CAVE OF THE HANDS
ARGENTINA

ART IN NATURE

Rock art is bound to the natural land-
scape. It is exposed to rain, sun, and ice.
Even though cave art is somewhat
protected from the weather, all rock flakes
and crumbles over time. In recent years,
fires, vandalism, tourists, and acid rain
caused by industry have damaged rock
art worldwide. Luckily, Cave of the Hands
was named a UNESCO World Heritage
site, which gives it international attention
and protection.

▲

Cave of the Hands, province of Santa Cruz,
Argentina, about 11,000–7,000 BCE

This portion of the wall shows handprints, animals,
and symbols.

Rio Pinturas Canyon

4

The big question is: Why did they do it? The answer is: We will never know—but we can make some educated guesses. As it happens, handprints are the most common subject for rock art and can be found worldwide. Like a signature or a tag, a handprint can declare "I was here." If the handprint was made as part of a religious ritual, it might say, "I have contacted the supernatural, or spirit, world." In the case of the handprints in Cave of the Hands, the fact that they were made in the same place for thousands of years might mean they were part of a tradition, perhaps something like a coming-of-age ceremony.

Rock art is the oldest visible form of human expression. For tens of thousands of years, people have drawn on cave ceilings and walls, cliffs, and desert rocks. Some drawings were made with paint; others were engraved, scraped, polished, or pecked into the stone. Each mark is a unique connection to our shared past.

Directions to the Afterworld

QUEEN NEFERTARI'S TOMB
EGYPT

Where do you go when you die? If you were an ancient Egyptian, you probably believed you went on a long journey to Eternity. But how would you know how to get there? In the spectacular tomb of Queen Nefertari, the directions are literally painted on the walls.

From her early teens until her death around the age of forty, Queen Nefertari was the first and favorite wife of the powerful pharaoh Ramses the Great. She had many honorary titles, including "Mistress of Upper and Lower Egypt" and "Lady of Charm." She may have been the only Egyptian queen to have a temple dedicated to her, which gave her the status of a goddess. When she died in 1255 BCE, she was buried in the largest and most beautiful tomb ever to be found in Egypt's Valley of the Queens.

Nefertari's "House of Eternity" contains two underground levels. Beneath star-covered ceilings, brilliant wall murals depict the young queen with figures from the Egyptian Book of the Dead. All of the artwork and hieroglyphic text was meant to guide Nefertari at each step along her way to the afterworld.

Tomb of Nefertari, Luxor, Egypt, about 1250 BCE

▲

Senet was an ancient board game played by two people. But in a scene found near the entrance to Nefertari's tomb, the queen is shown playing against an invisible opponent, Fate, whom she must defeat to gain immortality in the hereafter.

In the upper chambers of the tomb, the paintings show the mummification of the queen's corpse. In the illustrations that follow, she is welcomed into the underworld by Nekhbet, the vulture goddess; Edjo, the cobra goddess; and other supernatural beings. She offers them gifts in exchange for powers to help her on her perilous journey. She descends into the burial chamber, where she must pass through five gates to reach the underworld; each gate is guarded by three ferocious spirits. At the end of Nefertari's journey, Horus, the sun god, restores her body so she can be united with Osiris, god of the dead and ruler of the underworld.

Ancient craftsmen worked by the dim glow of oil lamps to make these tomb paintings. As soon as an area was dug out, workers applied layers of plaster to smooth the surface of the walls. A draftsman sketched onto the dried plaster in red paint. His boss then made corrections in black paint. Next, the plaster was modeled so that the figures stood out slightly from the walls. Finally, an artist painted the imagery with tempera paint against a white background. The high-relief paintings in Queen Nefertari's tomb are unmatched by those in any other tomb of the period.

SALT CRYSTALS

In 1904, Queen Nefertari's tomb was redis-covered by an Italian Egyptologist. After that, damage from natural forces and moisture from the breath of throngs of visitors began to threaten the paintings. From 1986 to 1992, Egyptian authorities teamed up with the Getty Conservation Institute to see what could be done. Studies found that cracking and flaking stone beneath the plaster allowed salt crystals to form when moisture was present. This was causing the plaster to blister and peel away. Emergency efforts were taken to stabilize and clean the tomb paintings. Today, the internal climate is carefully monitored and only a limited number of visitors are allowed inside to help the paintings last into the future.

GRAVE ROBBERS

Ancient Egyptian tombs were built to protect the bodies and belongings of the dead for eternity. To rob a grave was considered a terrible crime because it was thought to prevent the deceased from reaching the afterlife. Pharaohs hid their tombs, posted guards, blocked passageways with rubble, and had their burial chambers dug deep into the earth.

Still, most tombs were eventually looted. Within only a few years of Queen Nefertari's death, robbers plundered her burial chambers and may have searched her remains for gold and jewelry. They left little behind: a piece of a gold bracelet, several scarabs, a pair of sandals, fragments of her sarcophagus, a few figurines, and the queen's mummified knees.

Girl Power

MITHILA KOHBAR

INDIA

Throughout history, women artists were under-valued and overlooked. Most art training, travel, and trade were available only to men. But in the Mithila region of northern India, women invented an art form all their own, and they passed it down from woman to girl across generations.

Since very ancient times, women in the region created imaginative paintings on the walls and floors of their homes. Some people believe the practice started twenty-five hundred years ago, inspired by a story from the Ramayana, an epic poem written in Sanskrit. According to legend, King Janaka of Mithila held a contest to find a husband for his daughter, Sita. Five thousand men carried the heavy bow of the god Shiva into a room; the suitor who could lift and string the bow by himself would win Sita's hand. Prince Rama not only lifted the bow but also caused it to snap in two! To celebrate Sita's wedding to Rama, the king ordered murals to be painted throughout the palace. This story remains a popular subject for Mithila paintings.

Traditionally, a Mithila girl learned to draw and paint at a very young age. Then, days before her wedding, she showed her skill by decorating the marriage chamber, or *kohbar ghar*, with murals. She used whatever materials were available, for example, coal mixed with cow urine or gum arabic and water or goat milk. Her brush was a piece of straw, a twig, or a few threads pulled from the hem of her sari. The earliest painters used black from soot, red from local clay, and yellow from carnation pollen. The paints were not durable and the climate was humid, so the paintings soon faded away. Which was fine, because the murals weren't meant to last. Kohbar paintings are a form of prayer and meditation for the artist; it is the act of creating them that is important.

Although today some Mithila artists paint scenes from modern life, most of the subject matter is still inspired by traditional stories centered around Hindu deities such as Vishnu, Kali, Durgha, and Parvati. However, the materials used by the artists have

changed. In the mid-1960s, the region was struck by a devastating drought. Several women began using modern paints on paper, and they sold their work to earn badly needed income. They became the primary wage earners for their families and won respect within their communities. Some earned recognition and national awards from the Indian government.

More recently, this art form has become a tool of empowerment for women. Some Mithila artists express their ideas and comment on social issues through their work. Many use their income to improve their living conditions and to send their daughters to school. The Mithila style is recognized internationally, and exquisite examples can be found in museums and galleries around the world.

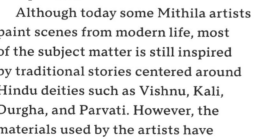

ART AS EXPERIENCE

Art is not just about the final product—it's also about the process itself. Many people find that making art is entertaining, relaxing, and enjoyable. It's something they do for themselves, whether they are good at it or not. The magic is that every person's work is completely unique. So, the next time you feel bored or stressed, try picking up a pencil or brush and discover the joy of making something only you can create.

Durga by Sita Devi,
Bihar, India, about 1973

SITA DEVI

Artist Sita Devi was one of the first to transfer this traditional art form from wall to paper, bringing international attention to Mithila painting. The above painting on paper shows the multi-armed goddess Durga seated on a lion.

Out of the Ashes

HERCULANEUM
ITALY

During ancient Roman times, Mount Vesuvius overlooked orchards and vineyards, busy towns, and elegant villas next to a sparkling blue bay. Until one day in late summer or early fall of 79 CE, when Vesuvius—an active volcano—erupted. People watched in amazement as a column of ash rose ten miles into the air, gradually cloaking the sky in darkness. Residents of Herculaneum, a small city at the foot of the mountain, grabbed what they could and raced for the harbor. Some escaped. Others huddled near the shore, hoping for a rescue that never came. Volcanic ash and debris up to sixty-five feet deep buried the entire town, essentially erasing it.

Sixteen centuries later, in 1709, a farmer digging a well unearthed some pieces of colored marble that had once adorned an ancient Roman theater.

A wealthy prince quickly purchased the surrounding land and hired laborers to tunnel down into the ruins, where they found more carved stone and some beautiful ancient statues. The prince used the valuable marble in the construction of his new villa. In 1738, King Charles VII of Naples began a large excavation of the buried city. His workmen cut fragments of murals out of Herculaneum's walls and installed them in a museum inside his nearby palace.

Today, archaeologists are working to uncover, study, and preserve the town of Herculaneum in its original location—including its many wall paintings. Fresco painting was a popular technique that involved applying paint to wet plaster so that, as the materials dried together, they both became part of the wall.

Frescoes decorated public and private spaces, beautifying walls and brightening dark, cramped rooms. If a home was too small to have a garden, a picture of one might be painted on a wall. Sometimes Roman wall paintings showed scenes from daily life, including traders selling their wares, people begging for money, or children studying from wax tablets. Other paintings recounted myths or depicted recently deceased rulers as gods. Each mural that emerges from the buried city reveals something new about the ancient Romans who once lived in the shadow of Vesuvius.

▼
Wall frescoes in the College of
the Augustales, Herculaneum, Italy,
before 79 CE

STYLES OF THE TIMES

Over the years, Roman frescoes developed into four styles.
Roman houses often contained a combination of these.

The earliest Roman wall frescoes
featured painted blocks that
mimicked expensive marble
slabs.

A newer approach used realistic,
three-dimensional images of
everyday objects and scenery.

After that, a more decorative
and less realistic style became
fashionable. Large walls were
broken up by fanciful painted
columns and frames surrounding
two-dimensional images.

By the time Vesuvius erupted,
painters were combining all of
these different styles.

Along the Silk Road

MOGAO GROTTOES

CHINA

According to legend, in 366 CE a Buddhist monk named Yuezun stood in front of the cliffs in Mogao, China, and saw a golden vision of a thousand radiant Buddhas. He was inspired to dig a cave into the cliffside to be used for spiritual meditation. Other monks, religious pilgrims, and wealthy families followed his example and had their own caves carved at Mogao. They hoped to create good karma—positive consequences of worthy deeds in this life and the next. Eventually, nearly five hundred decorated caves and niches honeycombed the half-mile cliff face. They became known as the Mogao Grottoes. People adorned their caves with beautiful murals and sculptures, making the Mogao Grottoes the largest collection of Buddhist art in the world.

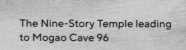

The Nine-Story Temple leading to Mogao Cave 96

19

Ceiling of Cave 205,
Dunhuang, China,
early Tang dynasty
(618–907 CE)

These Buddha figures
were hand painted
without pouncing or
stencils.

HOW TO MAKE A THOUSAND BUDDHAS

Many of Mogao's caves feature the
thousand-Buddha motif. In some
cases, the figures were hand painted
one by one; in others, artists made
sketches on paper and transferred
their designs onto the walls by
pouncing—dabbing charcoal or chalk
through tiny holes pricked into the
paper. Some artists used stencils
when they wanted to repeat the same
design—sometimes hundreds of
times.

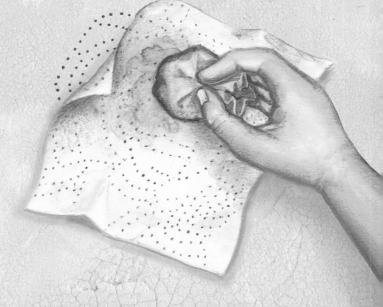

THE SILK ROAD

The Silk Road was an ever-changing series of routes used for hundreds of years by traders (of silk, spices, and other goods) and pilgrims traveling between ancient China and Europe. Dunhuang, the nearest town to the Mogao Grottoes, was a vital oasis along the Silk Road. It was a happening place where many cultures of the world—Chinese, Mongolian, Tibetan, Indian, Arab, Persian, Jewish, Greek, Roman, and others—came together.

In the end, Yuezun's vision came true: the caves contain well over a thousand images of the Buddha.

The Mogao Grottoes and the nearby town of Dunhuang used to be popular stops along the Silk Road. Weary travelers paused here to rest, trade, and pray for a safe journey through the high mountain passes and brutal deserts that lay ahead. But as time went on, fewer and fewer people passed through Dunhuang and Mogao. Eventually, fierce desert sandstorms blocked the cave entrances, and the site was mostly forgotten. But not forever. In the 1890s, Wang Yuanlu, a wandering Taoist priest, appointed himself unofficial guardian of the caves. One day, as he was sweeping sand from the entrance to Cave 16, he spied a doorway that had been plastered over and painted shut.

Breaking through the plaster, Wang discovered a hidden library with the original sketches for the caves, along with the world's oldest printed book and tens of thousands of other ancient manuscripts. His discovery attracted the attention of foreign adventurers, and some of Mogao's treasures were taken beyond China's borders, but the murals remained. If not for the remote setting and dry climate, the spectacular cave art of Mogao might have been lost to vandalism or decay. Today, conservation professionals from around the world are working to preserve it for future generations.

Ghouls and Princes

QUSAYR 'AMRA

JORDAN

A small, abandoned castle sits beside a cemetery in the middle of a windswept desert. Legend claims it is home to a ghoul, or jinn, that haunts desolate places. Fierce Bedouin raiding parties once roamed the area. No wonder Qusayr ʻAmra lay empty and nearly forgotten for almost twelve hundred years.

Yet, despite centuries of exposure to sandstorms, occasional rains, smoky campfires, and graffiti scratchers, parts of the royal site are in surprisingly good shape. The reception hall, throne room, baths, boiler, and hydraulic system are still standing. In fact, Qusayr ʻAmra is one of the best preserved and most impressive of the Umayyad palaces.

In the eighth century CE, followers of Islam conquered lands across the Middle East and constructed mosques and palaces throughout their new empire. The first Islamic dynasty was the Umayyad caliphate. Qusayr ʻAmra was built in about 730 CE as a residence for an Umayyad prince, al-Walīd ibn Yazīd. But why was it set in such a remote location? To find the answer, we turn to the murals and painted texts still visible on the walls.

In the reception hall, lavish murals depict men on horseback chasing a herd of gazelles into a netted trap. Long ago, large numbers of gazelles, onagers, hyenas, and even lions gathered to drink from a

nearby wadi, a seasonal water channel shaded by terebinth trees. At Qusayr 'Amra, the prince and his guests could return from a day of hunting to bathe, feast, and be entertained. Cool, warm, and hot baths—supplied with water by a system of wells and pipes—awaited the prince's weary hunting parties. The bath house was decorated with colorful murals and mosaics. It was a luxurious place for relaxing and enjoying music and refreshments.

Elsewhere in the palace is a mural of the prince himself, flanked by two servants. Another wall painting shows six world rulers honoring the Umayyad prince; it was designed to convey his status and power to all who entered his opulent desert dwelling.

A MAP OF THE HEAVENS

The painting on the ceiling of the Qusayr 'Amra caldarium (hot room) is special because it is the earliest known star map to be painted on the inside of a dome. Though deterioration makes it hard to see today, the mural includes symbols for about thirty-five constellations and four hundred stars.

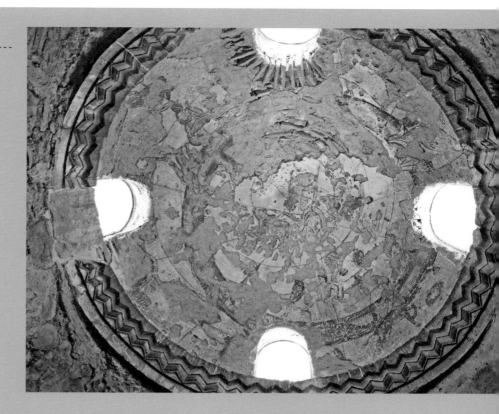

▶

Zodiac Dome, Qusayr 'Amra, Jordan, about 723–43 CE

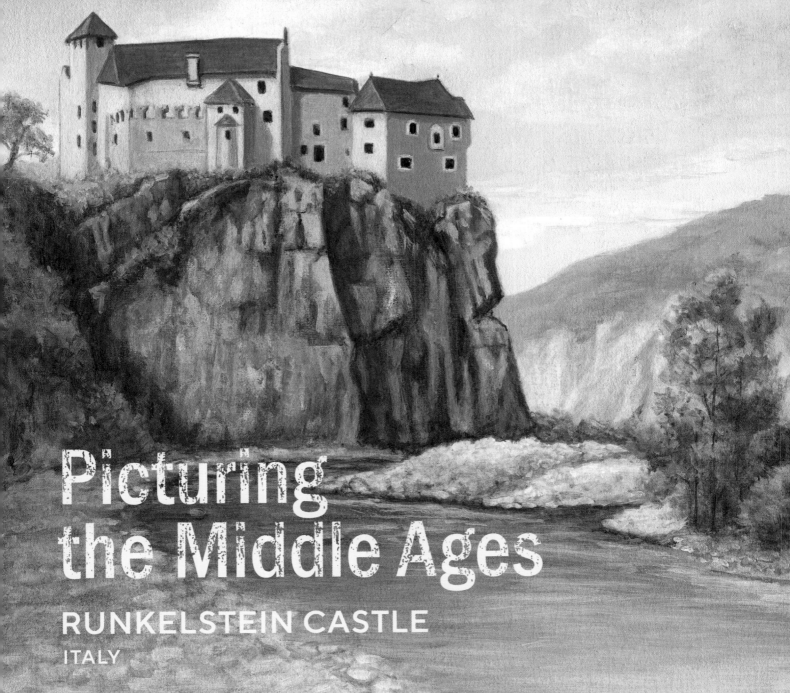

Picturing the Middle Ages

RUNKELSTEIN CASTLE
ITALY

The lore of the European Middle Ages was filled with knights, ladies, castles, dragons, and magic. These stories come to life on the walls of majestic Runkelstein Castle, perched atop a cliff in what is now Italy, close to the Austrian border. Built around 1237, the castle was purchased in 1385 by two brothers, Niklaus and Franz Vintler, who decorated the walls—inside and out—with murals.

Some of the colorful scenes are based on legendary tales, such as those of King Arthur and his knights gathered at the Round Table. One series tells the tragic Celtic love story of Tristan and Isolde, in which the knight Tristan slays a dragon and wins the hand of Princess Isolde for his uncle, King Mark. But Tristan and Isolde accidentally drink a love potion together, after

which they can't bear to be parted, and drama and adventure ensue.

Other frescoes celebrate court life, fashion, and popular sports. In the Tournament Room, a mural depicts knights wielding lances and trying to unseat their rivals from their horses. In the mural below it, on the left, lords and ladies await the toss of a ball to begin a game; to the right, young nobles dressed in high fashion join in a dance called the ridda.

Interestingly, the Vintlers themselves were not nobles; they came from a family of merchants and may have commissioned these murals to associate themselves with heroes, legends, and royalty.

▲
Tournament Room, Runkelstein Castle, Bolzano, Italy, about 1385

▶
Battle of Tristan against the Dragon, Runkelstein Castle, Bolzano, Italy, about 1385

Vintler coat of arms

Sculpted in Paint

SISTINE CHAPEL
VATICAN CITY

In the early 1500s, Pope Julius II summoned Italian sculptor Michelangelo to the Vatican in Rome. He wanted the artist to paint the ceiling of the Sistine Chapel. Michelangelo said no.

He had good reasons. The ceiling was five stories up and oddly shaped, with thousands of square feet of surface to cover. The job would take years, and Michelangelo preferred to spend his time sculpting, not painting. The pope wouldn't take no for an answer. Reluctantly, Michelangelo agreed to the project. Rival artists were certain he would fail. Instead, he rose to the challenge—literally.

To reach the ceiling, he designed a special wooden platform hung on brackets near the tops of the windows. Before ascending, he drew a cartoon of each scene on a large sheet of paper. The mural would be seen from far below and at odd angles, so he exaggerated the figures, often showing them in heroic and foreshortened poses. At first, he transferred his sketches to the freshly applied plaster by piercing the drawn lines with tiny holes and pouncing the paper with bags of charcoal powder. Later, he drew freely onto the plaster or painted without any sketches at all. He had spent a lifetime studying human anatomy for his sculptures, and he used this knowledge to design more than three hundred figures. To observers, it seemed like he was sculpting with paint.

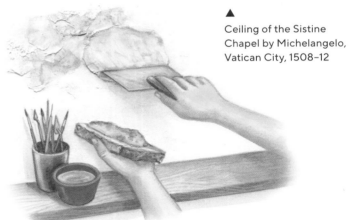

▲
Ceiling of the Sistine Chapel by Michelangelo, Vatican City, 1508–12

When he was done, stories from the Bible's book of Genesis filled nine central panels, framed by false concrete moldings and paintings of statues. In the triangles above each arched window were prophets and biblical figures. The Sistine Chapel ceiling is now considered one of the greatest achievements in European art.

TRICKS TO FOOL THE EYE

Trompe l'oeil is a technique used by artists to create optical illusions. Why? For architectural details like marble columns, for example, it is less expensive to paint pictures of them on walls than to carve real ones from stone.

Trompe l'oeil, a French term meaning "fool the eye," is a style of painting that may use a full range of colors to make the viewer believe that a painted object is real. On the ceiling of the Sistine Chapel, figures sit on realistic pedestals and are separated by "carved stone" frames. These sculptures and architectural details are actually painted optical illusions.

▶ Section of the ceiling of the Sistine Chapel by Michelangelo, Vatican City, 1508–12

History in Relief

PALACE ART OF ABOMEY

REPUBLIC OF BENIN

The fierce warrior kings of Dahomey were said to be descended from a princess and a legendary leopard. As rulers of the Fon people, they waged wars of conquest that expanded their territory with each generation. Eventually, Dahomey became one of the most powerful kingdoms in Africa. Its capital was Abomey where, beginning in 1645, every new king constructed his own palace out of rich red earth. Together, the palaces formed a large compound where royalty lived, ruled, and held lavish ceremonies.

Dahomey society had no written language, so its history was passed down through storytelling, dance, music, and art. For hundreds of years, the kings decorated their palace walls with sculpted and

Bas-relief from King Guezo's palace showing a warrior planting a flag on conquered territory, Abomey, Republic of Benin, mid-1800s

painted images, or bas-reliefs, that used pictograms to record glorious victories, epic tales, and cultural traditions.

Women in Dahomey society could become potters and sculptors. They could also join an elite group of female warriors and charge into battle. However, only men belonging to a special guild of artisans were allowed to create the royal bas-reliefs.

To form the three-dimensional wall art, earth was collected from termite mounds that were sometimes as tall as a person. Artists mixed the clay soil, which had been loosened by termites, with fibers and palm oil residue. Then, they applied this mixture to the walls and modeled it in place. After the mixture dried, they painted it with vibrant pigments made from local plants and minerals.

In 1892, the French colonial army marched into Abomey. King Behanzin, facing defeat, could not bear to see

Termite mound

SYMBOLS WITH MEANING

Every king of Dahomey had his own symbols and motto.

King Houegbadja
(reigned about 1645–85)

"The fish who has escaped the net will not go back in it."

King Akaba
(reigned 1685–1708)

"Slowly, patiently, the chameleon reaches the top of the kapok tree."

King Agonglo
(reigned 1789–97)

"Lightning strikes the palm tree but never the pineapple plant, which is close to the earth."

King Guezo
(reigned 1818–58)

"The powerful buffalo crosses the country and nothing can stop or confront it."

the palaces of his ancestors fall into enemy hands. Before fleeing, he ordered the structures set on fire. The palaces' thatched roofs were consumed by the flames. Left to the elements, the walls, along with their bas-relief murals, began to dissolve slowly back into the earth.

It took nearly seven decades for the Fon people to regain their independence from France. By then, some of the original structures had been lost. But now, within the modern Republic of Benin, the surviving palaces have been restored or reconstructed. The original bas-reliefs from the palace of King Glélé received conservation treatment and were placed inside a museum for their protection. These bas-reliefs are considered historical archives of the Fon culture. Local artists created replicas of the bas-reliefs to put on the reconstructed walls. Today, the palace complex is a center of Fon culture. The bas-reliefs not only honor a people's heritage but also continue to inspire the art of Benin.

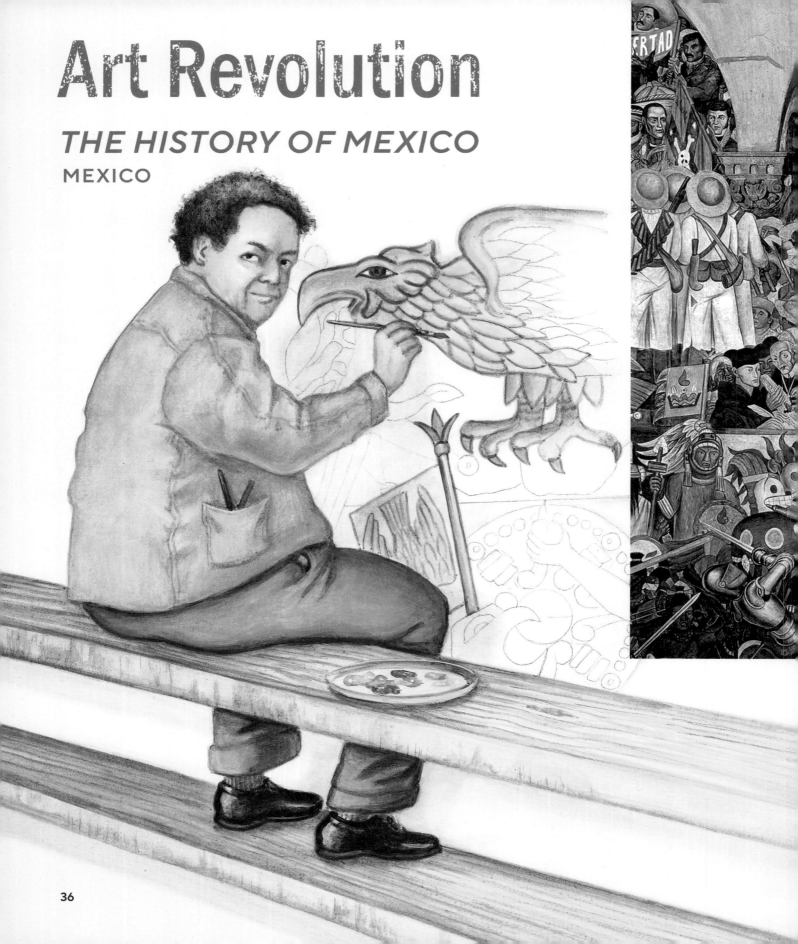

Art Revolution

THE HISTORY OF MEXICO

MEXICO

Section of *The History of Mexico* by Diego Rivera, National Palace, Mexico City, Mexico, 1929–35

Diego Rivera stood over six feet tall, but that's not why he was considered one of Los Tres Grandes (The Big Three). With fellow painters José Clemente Orozco and David Alfaro Siqueiros, he launched the first art movement to come out of the Americas in the twentieth century: Mexican muralism. Forged in the embers of the Mexican Revolution, this intense style of public art would become a tool for change throughout the world.

When Rivera was a young man, Mexico was plagued by corruption, poverty, and prejudice against Indigenous and mestizo (mixed-race) people. In 1910, the people rose up, and the revolution that followed lasted more than a decade. During this time, Rivera went to Europe to study the work of world-famous artists such as

The Making of a Fresco Showing the Building of a City by Diego Rivera,
San Francisco Art Institute, United States, 1931

LOS TRES GRANDES

Diego Rivera, José Clemente Orozco, and David Alfaro Siqueiros were called Los Tres Grandes, or The Big Three. Although they never worked together, they led the Mexican muralist movement. Its revolutionary influence changed the style and social impact of art throughout the world.

Self-portrait by José Clemente Orozco, 1937

José Clemente Orozco became an important painter despite losing his left hand at the age of twenty-one while making fireworks with gunpowder for Mexican Independence Day. He was the oldest of The Big Three and had experienced much of the Mexican Revolution himself. He intended his art to help poor and suffering people and to call for change. "The highest, the most logical, the purest and strongest form of painting is the mural. In this form…it cannot be hidden away for the benefit of a certain privileged few. It is for the people. It is for ALL."

Michelangelo and Picasso. While away he realized something: "What I knew best and felt most deeply was my own country." When he returned home, Rivera was eager to create a new art form, one that would "reflect the social life of Mexico as I saw it." Art of this kind would come to be called social realism. Rivera wanted to celebrate Indigenous people, promote the rights of all workers, and create a sense of optimism for his beloved homeland. Such big goals needed a lot of room, and murals on large walls became his preferred medium.

One of Rivera's larger-than-life masterpieces lines the stairwell of the National Palace in Mexico City. In it the artist featured new kinds of heroes—Aztec warriors battling Spanish conquistadors, peasants fighting in the revolution, hardworking farmers feeding the nation, people of all races building a new Mexico. It celebrates common people instead of the rich and powerful.

In 1931, the San Francisco Art Institute invited Rivera to paint a mural and offered him 120 square feet of wall space. But, as he said later, "I chose another wall, ten times as big." He insisted on more room to picture the many technicians, planners, and artists who had to work together to create a modern city. The mural celebrates all kinds of laborers, including Rivera himself as a muralist painting a mural about making murals. You can see him in the middle, facing away from the viewer, wearing blue pants and a yellow shirt.

Diego Rivera died in 1957. To this day, he is remembered as a Mexican national treasure and one of the most significant figures in the history of art.

David Alfaro Siqueiros was the youngest and most radical of The Big Three. He dedicated his life to demanding change through public art—even when it cost him jobs or landed him in jail. He said, "Art…should aim to become a fighting educative art for all." The artist was known not just for his revolutionary thinking but also for his revolutionary techniques: he liked to use airbrushes, spray guns, pre-colored cement, and blowtorches to make his murals.

Self-portrait by David Alfaro Siqueiros, 1945

A New Deal for Public Art

COIT TOWER MURALS
UNITED STATES

The Great Depression began in 1929 and caused poverty around the world. Many artists fell on hard times. As part of the New Deal—US president Franklin D. Roosevelt's plan to help the country recover—the Public Works of Art Project (PWAP) was formed to provide jobs for artists. Today, magnificent murals by PWAP painters still grace libraries, post offices, schools, and other public buildings throughout the United States.

The largest PWAP project is inside Coit Tower, a 212-foot-tall monument atop Telegraph Hill in San Francisco. The structure is a memorial to Lillian "Firebelle" Coit, a supporter of the local fire department who also bequeathed funds for the beautification of the city. Ironically, she never wanted a memorial or even liked towers!

Twenty-five artists, including four women, were hired by the PWAP to paint murals inside the building. The theme was "Contemporary Aspects of Life in California." To create a unified appearance, one assistant mixed all the colors, and all the muralists were asked to adopt the style and techniques of Diego

Greetings from Coit Tower

San Francisco, California

Rivera. Many also selected themes inspired by Rivera's murals, such as economic inequality and workers' rights.

Some of the artists knew Rivera personally. Maxine Albro studied fresco at his studio in Mexico. Rivera invited Jewish artist Bernard Zakheim to visit him in Mexico City. Rivera admired Zakheim's drawings of Jewish life and remarked that "every artist puts into his work something...of his own people."

Coit Tower opened its doors on October 20, 1934. It is still considered an important cultural landmark today.

California by Maxine Albro, San Francisco, United States, 1934

This Coit Tower mural celebrates the farmworkers who pick flowers and oranges under the hot California sun.

▶
Library by Bernard Zakheim, San Francisco, United States, 1934

The people, books, and newspapers depicted by Zakheim in his Coit Tower mural reflect his political and religious beliefs.

Justice and Remembrance

AMISTAD MURALS
UNITED STATES

In the early hours of June 28, 1839, the Spanish ship *Amistad* set sail from Havana, Cuba, bound for the town of Puerto Príncipe, farther down the coast. Chained belowdecks were forty-nine men and four children who had been abducted in West Africa. They were to be enslaved and forced to work on Cuba's new sugar plantations.

On their fourth night at sea, the Black captives escaped their shackles, killed the captain and a cook, and took control of the ship. They demanded to be returned to their homes across the ocean.

But the remaining Spanish sailors tricked them, traveling east by day but turning north by night. The *Amistad* was seized near New York, and thirty-six of the men were locked in jail and put on trial for piracy and murder. A fierce public debate followed: Should the captured Africans be found guilty, or did they deserve the same rights as free men to defend themselves and choose their own destiny?

The case went all the way to the US Supreme Court, where attorney Roger Baldwin and former president John Quincy Adams argued on behalf of the *Amistad* prisoners. At the time, enslavement was still legal in America, but international trade in human beings had been banned by treaties between Spain, the United States, and other

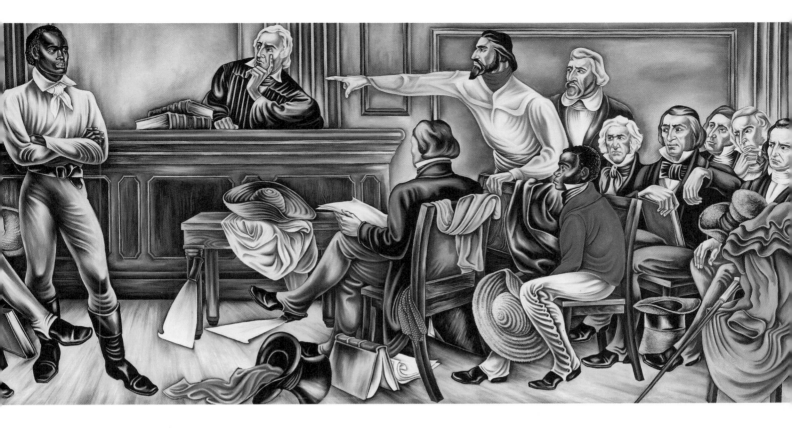

The Trial of the Amistad Captives by Hale Woodruff, Talladega, United States, 1939

Look closely and you can see a self-portrait of the artist: he is sitting in the third row, his chin resting on his hand.

◀

The Repatriation of the Freed Captives by Hale Woodruff, Talladega, United States, 1939

countries. At the end of a long trial, the court declared the Africans to be free people. In November 1841, the remaining survivors of the *Amistad* uprising returned to their homelands.

Their victory was big news at the time, but it was hardly mentioned in twentieth-century history books. However, at Talladega College, Alabama's oldest private Black liberal arts college, people remembered. To mark the 100th anniversary of the *Amistad* uprising, the college invited African American artist Hale Woodruff to illustrate the series of events on panels for its new Savery Library. The *Amistad* murals—the largest of which is more than twenty feet long— are some of the most important artworks to come out of the social realist mural movement of the 1930s and '40s.

Woodruff was already well known for his pictures of African American life in the segregated South when he won a fellowship to train with Diego Rivera. He returned from Mexico even more determined to shine a light on racial injustice. His grand *Amistad* murals remind the world about a long-ago victory in the ongoing struggle for equality.

MURALS OR PAINTINGS?

Woodruff painted the *Amistad* murals on gigantic canvases in his studio—for a good reason. Years before, he had painted some murals directly on the walls for a library at Atlanta University. Later, a librarian who didn't like them threatened to paint over them! Woodruff wanted the *Amistad* murals to be removable in case this happened again. Although he always called his *Amistad* paintings murals, some might say they are paintings, since they weren't painted directly on the walls. What do you think?

One of the longest paintings in the world doesn't fit inside a museum or a mansion—it lines a concrete flood channel that is part of the Los Angeles River. The half-mile mural is titled *The History of California*, but almost everyone calls it The Great Wall of Los Angeles. It began in 1974 as a public project led by artist and activist Judy Baca, who trained at the muralism workshop founded by David Alfaro Siqueiros. Baca's mural illustrates the cultural, political, and natural history of her home state—from the Stone Age through the 1950s. She has described The Great Wall as the "recovery of our river and the story of how we came to be where we are."

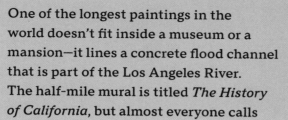

Tattoo for a River

THE GREAT WALL OF LOS ANGELES
UNITED STATES

The mural highlights the histories of often marginalized people, including Native Americans, Mexican Americans, African Americans, immigrants, women, and the LGBTQ+ community. It celebrates unsung heroes like abolitionist Mary Ellen Pleasant and Medal of Honor recipient David M. Gonzales. It marks milestones such as the discovery of gold and the birth of rock and roll. And it shines a light on dark episodes from the past, including the Chinese Massacre of 1871 and the plight of Jewish refugees fleeing the Holocaust.

From the beginning, Baca saw the trash-strewn and graffitied drainage trench as an opportunity to transform an eyesore into a treasure. She called on poets, artists, and historians to help her envision each section of the mural, and she blended the sections together visually using triangles, sweeping lines, and subjects in motion.

To create the immense mural, Baca hired people between the ages of fourteen and twenty-one. Several were taggers, and many were affiliated with rival gangs. All had been arrested at least once. Over six summers between 1976 and 1984, four hundred young people and thirty-five artists put in seventy-five thousand hours to apply seven hundred gallons of paint to a wall that stretched more than six city blocks. The young mural makers worked together to transfer one-by-two-foot blueprints to thirteen-foot-high walls, erect scaffolding, and cope with flash floods and temperatures over one hundred degrees Fahrenheit.

In Baca's own words, The Great Wall is now a "tattoo on the scar where the river once ran." And now with new funding, work on the mural will continue. When completed in 2028, The Great Wall of Los Angeles will stretch a mile long and depict the Golden State's past from prehistory to the present and beyond.

▲
Prehistoric California
by Judith F. Baca,
Los Angeles,
United States, 1976

TOOLS AND MATERIALS

Turning a concrete flood channel into a work of art was not easy. Each area to be painted was blasted with sand and then with water to smooth the surface before being primed with white gesso. Next, a grid was chalked onto the wall. Using this grid, artists painted sketches in blue one square at a time. Then a magenta undercoat was applied to blend all the colors and cut the glare from the white wall. Each panel had its own base color. Muralists first painted large areas of flat color and then added dark shading and highlights. Scumbling, or overpainting lightly with a dry brush, allowed the layers of color to show through. The mural was sealed with a clear acrylic coating to protect it from sun, pollution, and graffiti.

▼

The Birth of Rock and Roll by Judith F. Baca, Los Angeles, United States, 1983

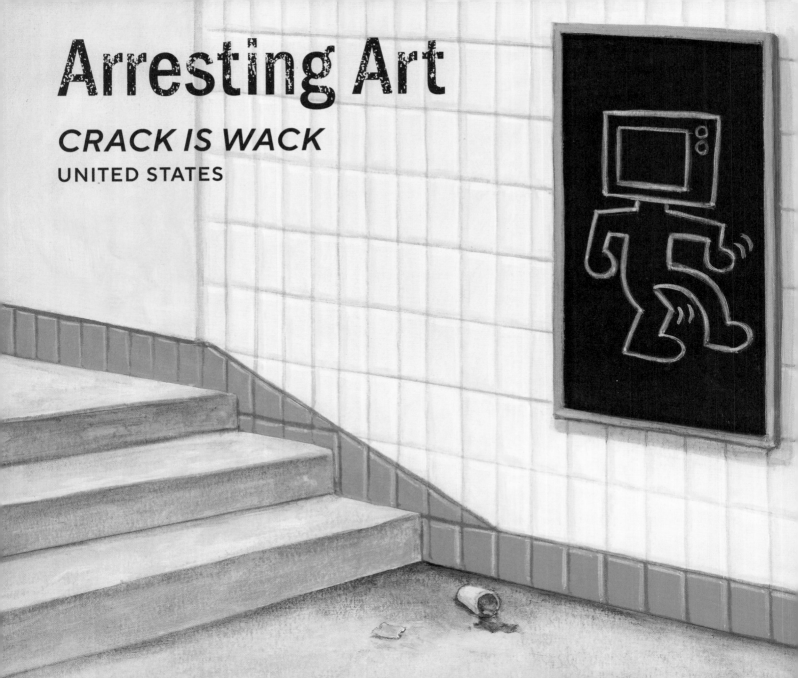

Arresting Art

CRACK IS WACK
UNITED STATES

When Keith Haring was a child in Kutztown, Pennsylvania, he and his father would lie on the floor and take turns drawing lines on the same piece of paper. The lines would morph into a dog, a fish, a man with a beach ball on his head, or something else that made them laugh.

As a young man in 1978, Haring enrolled in the School of Visual Arts in New York City. It was an exciting time when graffiti writers, musicians, performance artists, and others were bringing their work into the streets. Haring loved the idea of art for everybody everywhere—not just in museums. One day Haring was riding the subway when he noticed unused advertising panels covered in black paper. He rushed off to buy white chalk and came back to draw on the panels. The subway soon became his art laboratory, where he might make up to forty drawings a day. He experimented with cartoonlike symbols to express his feelings about relationships, life, death, and war. A dollar sign stood for greed,

a heart for love, a barking dog for abuse of power. A figure he called the Radiant Baby represented Haring himself. Subway riders enjoyed his pictures and were especially thrilled if they caught a glimpse of the mystery artist. Law enforcement took notice too and arrested Haring several times for drawing on walls without permission.

The traditional art world couldn't ignore Haring's talent forever. His work began to appear in galleries and museums, and he was invited to paint murals in countries around the globe. Some of his art was joyful and meant to make people smile. Some shared messages about important topics like racism and drug abuse. As an openly gay artist, Haring was concerned about a terrible epidemic spreading through his community, and AIDS awareness became an important theme in his art.

When his gifted assistant, Benny, became addicted to crack, Haring set out to paint a mural warning people about the dangerous drug. He found the perfect site for his *Crack Is Wack* mural on a handball court in a park along Harlem River Drive, passed by hundreds of cars every day. While Haring was completing the mural, a police officer arrested him for painting without permission. National attention brought a speedy end to his legal case, and he was released from jail with only a $25 fine.

After Haring died at age thirty-one from an AIDS-related illness, the park was officially renamed the Crack Is Wack Playground in his honor. His paintings continue to remind us of the power of art to create joy anywhere and to inspire change everywhere.

▶
Crack Is Wack by Keith Haring, New York City, United States, 1986

▼
We the Youth by Keith Haring, Philadelphia, United States, 1987

GRAFFITI

The word *graffito* is old Italian slang for "little mark," and ever since there have been humans and blank surfaces, people have left their marks on everything from prehistoric caves and tree bark to bathroom walls and freeway underpasses. The urge to tell the world "I was here" seems part of our nature.

In the late 1960s, a new kind of graffiti exploded in American cities. Taggers used spray paint to write their anonymous street names on subway cars, public buildings, and private property. For many it was a show of resistance to authority, racism, and poverty. It could display the writer's daring and earn the respect of other graffiti writers. It was also used by gangs to mark their territory. Sometimes graffiti was angry and ugly, sometimes skillful and creative. It was (and is) illegal and often very dangerous.

The hand lettering and bold styles of graffiti are still seen in art, advertising, design, and fashion today. Generations of artists have followed the path of Keith Haring and his friend Jean-Michel Basquiat from graffiti artists to celebrated painters. One lasting effect of the graffiti wave is that many people now recognize street art as a meaningful form of expression that, when created with the support of the community, can brighten up our world.

▼
Radiant Baby (from the Grace House mural) by Keith Haring, New York City, United States, 1983–84

It was a date Kani Alavi would never forget.

On November 9, 1989, the Iranian artist was living in Berlin, Germany. That day, he watched from the window of his fourth-floor apartment as thousands of citizens carrying picks and hammers rushed the Berlin Wall, intending to tear it down.

After Germany's 1945 defeat in World War II, the country was divided into two parts. West Germany was allied with the United States, France, and the United Kingdom and became an open society. East Germany was strictly controlled by the Soviet Union. The city of Berlin was also split in two. Some years later, the Soviet Union built a ninety-six-mile-long concrete wall to keep East German citizens from escaping into free West Berlin.

In 1989, an eruption of protests led East Germany to announce the opening of its borders. That November day, Alavi saw portions of the Berlin Wall crumble as waves of people surged toward liberty.

Wall of War and Peace

BERLIN WALL
GERMANY

PARIACHI | NOV·9-89

BIRGIT KINDER

Birgit K.
09.07.09

Soon after, 118 artists from around the world arrived to celebrate and also to preserve the story of the divided city on what was left of the wall. Alavi joined them in painting images of unity and freedom. The artists called their wall of murals the East Side Gallery. One of the artists was Birgit Kinder, who arrived from East Germany in her Trabant, a Communist-produced car. Kinder painted an image of her car smashing through the wall.

In 1991, the East Side Gallery was named a protected heritage site, but that didn't stop the destruction of several sections. Some were removed to make way for luxury apartments; others were taken down to allow access to a river pier. Tourists chipped away pieces to keep as souvenirs. Alavi played a key role in the effort to restore the paintings and preserve the gallery. Eventually, because walls can defend as well as divide, a fence was built to protect the wall. What remains of the Berlin Wall today shows how a reminder of oppression can be transformed by art into a symbol of perseverance and peace.

▶

It Happened in November by Kani Alavi, East Side Gallery, Berlin, Germany, 1990

▼

The Wall Jumper by Gabriel Heimler, East Side Gallery, Berlin, Germany, 1990

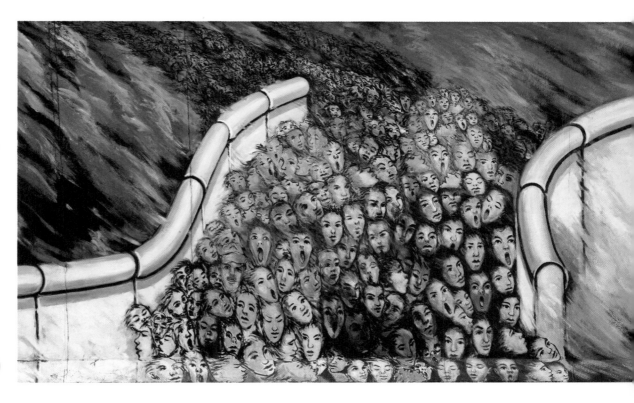

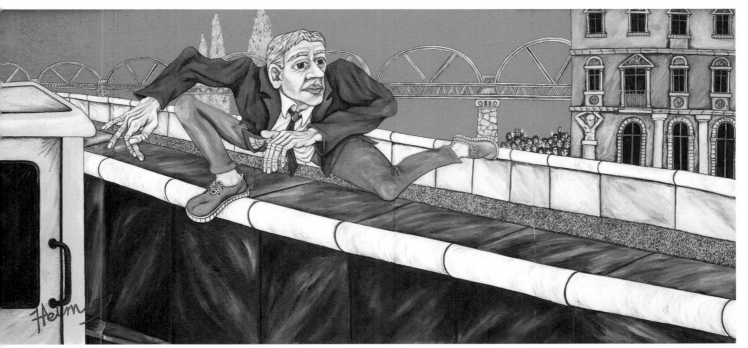

For the Birds

LILITH AND OLAF

NORWAY

Birds have the best view of *Lilith and Olaf.* Across connected rooftops spanning about 226,000 square feet, this enormous mural was created for the 2015 Nuart street art festival in Norway. It can also be seen by airline passengers, which is why planes taking off from Stavanger Airport began diverting their flight paths for a better view. Ella and Pitr, the French street artists who created the mural, are known for their quirky, absurdly large art pieces around the world—on rooftops, runways, open fields, shipping containers, and even in ink on snow.

Lilith and Olaf shows a snoozing woman in a tank top and running shorts, painted in shades of gray except for her red nails. She is one in a series of slumbering giants cramped in their sleeping spaces. Ella and Pitr suggest that they are perhaps "dreaming about another way to live. But also, we imagine that they could wake up sometime, and this idea is very awesome."

Lilith and Olaf by Ella and Pitr, Klepp, Norway, 2015

ANAMORPHOSIS

Like many of Ella and Pitr's works, *Lilith and Olaf* is an anamorphosis—a distorted drawing or painting that appears normal only when seen from a specific angle or location, or when using a special device. Since *Lilith and Olaf* occupies several connected rooftops of different heights, the painting only appears flat when seen from the sky overhead.

Ella and Pitr worked with a photographer and a technical lighting director to create the anamorphic image above. The piece may seem like a flat picture frame on a photo—but look closer. Ella and Pitr have actually painted the walls, ceiling, and floors of two rooms in an abandoned building. The illusion only works, though, when viewed from a specific location. Step to the side, and the frame and painted orange surfaces no longer line up correctly, and the illusion is broken.

▲
Photograph from a series for the Centre Dramatique by Ella and Pitr, Saint-Étienne, France, 2013–14

At Lilith's fingertips is a relatively small portrait of King Olaf I of Norway, who ruled from 995 to 1000 CE. Ella and Pitr were asked to include the monarch because he was born on an islet just a stone's throw away from the building. So why is the king so small? While researching, the couple discovered that King Olaf led violent raids and also tortured and killed people who refused to convert to Christianity. Because he treated people with cruelty, the artists transformed Olaf into a tiny plaything for Lilith.

It took Ella, Pitr, and their volunteers only four days to paint the massive mural. They are pleased that people can see it from planes flying overhead; they've said that viewing large-scale art this way makes the Earth seem not so big after all.

When Words Are Not Enough

DREAMING GRAFFITI

AFGHANISTAN

While living in war-torn Afghanistan in the 2010s, muralist Shamsia Hassani had to watch out for land mines and bombings as she created her work on walls. She was the first female graffiti and street artist in a country that severely limits women's freedoms. Though graffiti was legal in Afghanistan at the time, many people there did not approve of a girl coloring on the walls. Passersby sometimes shouted insults at her as she championed women's rights— using paint.

Graffiti at Dural Aman by Shamsia Hassani, Kabul, Afghanistan, 2014

Hassani studied fine art at Kabul University. But it was a graffiti workshop organized by Combat Communication including CHU, an artist from the United Kingdom, that sparked her love for street art. She realized that by painting outdoors on the bullet-riddled walls of abandoned buildings in Kabul, her images might become a part of people's everyday lives and, in her words, "color over the bad memories of war." It was a risky ambition, and she had to figure out how to work quickly. By using a few cans of spray paint and adding details with small brushes and acrylic paint, she found she could complete a painting in fifteen minutes. She painted women wearing traditional burqas or hijabs: strong, energetic women who dared to leave their homes and start their lives over. Few of Hassani's figures have mouths, but many have musical instruments, which she sees as tools to help women be heard.

▲
From the Nightmare series by Shamsia Hassani, 2021

This series marked the return of the Taliban to Afghanistan.

▶
From the Dreaming Graffiti series by Shamsia Hassani, 2023

Here Hassani added the image of a woman playing a keyboard to a photograph of Kabul, Afghanistan.

Hassani continued to travel and spread her art all around the world. She was not in Afghanistan when the Taliban, an Islamic fundamentalist group, returned to power in 2021. The Taliban condemned art as "un-Islamic" and began whitewashing murals. Fearing for her safety, Hassani did not return to her homeland. She said, "The day Kabul fell, I could not believe it; my heart was on fire." Now safe but far from her home country, the artist uses pictures of places that are important to her and adds graffiti to these photographs digitally or with a paintbrush. She calls this "dreaming graffiti." Like the women she still paints, Shamsia Hassani is a strong, proud leader of change who hopes her country will someday be known for its art, not its wars.

WOMEN ARTISTS BREAKING BOUNDARIES

Street art has historically been a male-dominated field, but there is a growing number of women artists who are taking to the walls to bring change. Laila Ajjawi, a Palestinian refugee in Jordan, paints murals on refugee camp walls. Her work focuses on equal rights for women, education, and poor camp conditions.

In Rio de Janeiro, Panmela Castro, also known as Brazil's graffiti queen, uses her art to fight gender stereotypes and bring awareness to domestic violence. Her portraits of female figures are an attempt to reclaim public spaces for women.

And in Quito, Ecuador, street artist Sofia Acosta, who goes by La Suerte (Luck), creates murals that address the female body. She said, "Here in Ecuador, dealing with body issues or talking about the body is still a sin." All three of these women—and others like them—believe that art on walls can bring change when words are not enough.

PRESERVING THE WORLD'S MURALS

By Leslie Rainer, wall paintings conservator and senior project specialist, Getty Conservation Institute

With the wealth of murals, both historical and modern, around the world comes the need to maintain and preserve them. Because murals are often outdoors—exposed to weather, pollution, and vandalism—conserving them can be a real challenge. Plaster detaching from the wall, paint flaking and falling off, pollution building up on the surface, and destructive graffiti are just a few of the possible problems. The buildings on which some art is painted can also be damaged by earthquakes, floods, and erosion.

The Getty Conservation Institute and other organizations and individuals across the globe are working to preserve murals. Professional mural or wall paintings conservators are trained in university graduate programs, through apprenticeships, and via field experience to address the many issues murals may face. However, due to the size, scale, and architectural context of these artworks, the experts rarely work alone. Teams include architects, engineers, documentation specialists, conservators, and community members. In fact, communities are essential to the long-term preservation of murals. The people who live with murals, who interact and connect with them, make a difference whether the artworks are in local historical churches, mosques, temples, or synagogues; on the walls of public buildings or shops; or on the exteriors of houses or apartment complexes. Communities can watch over murals and care for the landscapes around them. When they notice an issue, they can raise it with the building owner or authority, and a conservator can then carry out treatment.

Also essential to the preservation of murals are the artists who created them. When artists are still living and available, they can join forces with conservators. Artists can give guidance on their original intent and colors, and conservators can offer technical advice about things like cleaning surfaces or re-adhering flaking paint.

On archaeological sites, conservators collaborate with archaeologists and art historians to piece together information about the style and content of murals as well as the materials and techniques used to create them. Scientists play an important role too, helping to characterize materials and techniques and working with conservators to develop appropriate conservation treatments.

The interdisciplinary teams that conserve murals vary widely and are diverse; each team member specializes in a specific aspect of the job. Therefore, murals are best preserved when there is a holistic approach and a group effort to care for them at all levels.

▲

The Getty Conservation Institute partnered with the Dunhuang Academy to conserve the wall paintings in Cave 85 at the Mogao Grottoes in China (see page 19). The team developed innovative solutions for conservation, including reattaching earthen plaster to the walls and ceilings of the cave temple as a prototype for the conservation of the nearly 500 other decorated cave temple spaces at the site.

◄

The mural *América Tropical* was painted in downtown Los Angeles in 1932 by Mexican artist David Alfaro Siqueiros (see page 39). The work criticizes the treatment of Indigenous peoples "by the invaders of both yesterday and today," said the artist. Civic leaders who objected to the mural's content had it covered with whitewash, and it was neglected for decades. Since 1988, the Getty Conservation Institute and El Pueblo de Los Angeles Historical Monument have worked together to preserve the mural, protect it with a shelter, and provide visitors access to view it. Conservators removed whitewash, reattached loose plaster to the wall, cleaned the surface, and retouched areas of damage. El Pueblo museum staff will continue to monitor and care for the mural as stewards of the site.

AFTERWORD

WHAT'S NEXT?

As long as there are people and walls, there will be wall art. Some artists will continue to make murals in traditional ways. Others will pursue new technologies to push the boundaries of the possible. For example, some muralists are using animation and augmented reality to bring their art to life. Dutch artist Leon Keer collaborated with augmented reality designer Joost Spek to create a five-story-high mural of stacked teacups. When viewed using Spek's app, Keer's painted teacups appear to tumble and shatter. Some artists are making murals that require viewers to wear 3D glasses. Some employ projection mapping, a technique that uses several projectors to "wrap" images around irregularly shaped structures such as buildings. And after that, who knows?

▲
Shattering by Leon Keer, Helsingborg, Sweden, 2020

SELECTED SOURCES

BOOKS

Agnew, Neville, Marcia Reed, and Tevvy Ball, eds. *Cave Temples of Dunhuang: Buddhist Art on China's Silk Road.* Los Angeles: Getty Conservation Institute, 2016.

Clottes, Jean. *World Rock Art.* Los Angeles: Getty Conservation Institute, 2002.

Court, Sarah, and Leslie Rainer. *Herculaneum and the House of the Bicentenary: History and Heritage.* Los Angeles: Getty Conservation Institute, 2020.

Finlay, Victoria. *The Brilliant History of Color in Art.* Los Angeles: J. Paul Getty Museum, 2014.

Folgarait, Leonard. *Mural Painting and Social Revolution in Mexico, 1920–1940.* Cambridge: Cambridge University Press, 1998.

Fowden, Garth. *Qusayr 'Amra: Art and the Umayyad Elite in Late Antique Syria.* Berkeley: University of California Press, 2004.

Graham-Dixon, Andrew. *Michelangelo and the Sistine Chapel.* New York: Skyhorse, 2016.

Greco, Christian, et al. *Queen Nefertari's Egypt.* Fort Worth: Kimbell Art Museum, 2020.

Gruen, John. *Keith Haring: The Authorized Biography.* New York: Prentice Hall, 1991.

ACKNOWLEDGMENTS

In addition to writing and illustrating children's books, I have been a muralist for more than twenty years, so *Wall to Wall* was undeniably a labor of love, though it was not without its challenges—the COVID-19 pandemic, to name one. Were it not for the incredible enthusiasm, talent, patience, and perseverance of my editor and collaborator, Elizabeth Nicholson, none of it would have been possible. I will be forever grateful to her. I was then twice blessed with the thoughtful insights of Leslie Rainer, senior project specialist at the Getty Conservation Institute, who generously contributed her time and expertise.

I wish to give my heartfelt thanks to the many experts and educators who provided feedback at various stages of the book's development: Catherine Benkaim, Suzanne Blier, Madeline J. Bryant, Garth Fowden, Davide Gasparotto, Uma Krishnaswami, Kenneth Lapatin, Elizabeth Morrison, and Julie Paik. A special shout-out goes to Mrs. Paik's seventh-grade students at A. E. Wright Middle School in Calabasas, California, who enthusiastically provided their well-considered input.

Thank you to the incomparable Getty book team—Danielle Brink, Jeffrey Cohen, Michelle Deemer, and Kurt Hauser—who took my initial design ideas and honed them into a visual banquet. Thanks also to first-rate copy editor Amanda Sparrow. I also greatly appreciated the support of many others at Getty Publications, including Tevvy Ball, Clare Davis, Joanne Kenny, Kara Kirk, Darryl Oliver, and Maureen Winter.

Special thanks to my husband, Todd Fraser, for his endless patience throughout this project. During this journey to publication, he endured out-of-state moves, illness, travels, and my incessant musings on all things to do with painting on walls.

None of this, of course, would have been possible without the artists included in this volume. Their works illuminate our past, beg us to ask tough questions, and beautify our world.
—Mary Ann Fraser

Haring, Kay A. *Keith Haring: The Boy Who Just Kept Drawing.* New York: Dial Books for Young Readers, 2017.

Heydt, Stephanie Mayer. *Rising Up: Hale Woodruff's Murals at Talladega College.* Atlanta: High Museum of Art, 2012.

Knight, Margy Burns. *Talking Walls: Discover Your World.* Gardiner, ME: Tilbury House, 1992.

Levy, Patricia. *The Fall of the Berlin Wall: November 9, 1989.* London: Hachette Children's Group, 2019.

McDonald, John K. *House of Eternity: The Tomb of Nefertari.* Los Angeles: Getty Conservation Institute, 1996.

Medina, Nico. *What Was the Berlin Wall?* New York: Penguin Workshop, 2019.

Pietrangeli, Carlo, et al. *The Sistine Chapel: The Art, the History, and the Restoration.* New York: Harmony Books, 1986.

Piqué, Francesca, and Leslie H. Rainer. *Palace Sculptures of Abomey: History Told on Walls.* Los Angeles: Getty Conservation Institute, 1999.

Prehistoric Art: Cave Dwellers Edition. Newark, DE: Speedy, 2018.

Rochfort, Desmond. *Mexican Muralists.* San Francisco: Chronicle Books, 1993.

Rosen, Aaron. *A Journey through Art: A Global History.* London: Thames & Hudson, 2018.

Rubin, Susan Goldman. *Diego Rivera: An Artist for the People.* New York: Henry N. Abrams, 2013.

Stanley, Diane. *Michelangelo.* New York: HarperCollins, 2000.

Veronico, Nicholas A., et al. *Depression-Era Murals of the Bay Area.* Charleston, SC: Arcadia, 2014.

Zakheim, Masha. *Coit Tower San Francisco: Its History and Art.* San Francisco: Volcano Press, 2009.

WEBSITES

Ella and Pitr: https://www.designboom.com/art/ella-pitr-nuart-largest-mural-in-the-world-lilith-olaf-08-31-2015/; ellapitr.com

Getty Conservation Institute: https://www.getty.edu/conservation/

Great Wall of Los Angeles: http://www.judybaca.com/artist/; https://sparcinla.org

Shamsia Hassani: https://www.shamsiahassani.net

Mithila painting: https://orias.berkeley.edu/resources-teachers/mithila-painting-folk-art-india

Runkelstein Castle: https://www.runkelstein.info/home-english

United Nations Educational, Scientific and Cultural Organization (UNESCO): https://whc.unesco.org

GLOSSARY

AIRBRUSH—a device that uses compressed air to apply paint as a fine spray.

ANAMORPHOSIS—an image that appears distorted unless seen from a specific viewpoint or observed using a special device.

BAS-RELIEF—a kind of sculpture in which the image is raised from a flat background to give a three-dimensional effect.

BINDER—a substance that allows other materials to bond together, for example, by helping pigment to adhere to a wall.

BLOWTORCH—a small handheld burner.

BLUEPRINT—a photographic print, typically white on a bright blue ground or blue on a white ground, that is used especially for copying drawings and maps or for following architectural plans.

CARTOON—a preparatory drawing, painting, or design an artist makes before starting a fresco or other large artwork.

CAVE ART—artwork applied to the surface of a cave or a rock found in nature.

ENGRAVE—to carve an image or words into a surface of, for example, wood, metal, clay, or stone.

FORESHORTEN—to distort an image so that it appears as if an object or figure is projecting toward the viewer.

FRESCO—a painting on a wall or ceiling done in pigment on wet plaster so that the color becomes part of the plaster as it dries.

GESSO—a paste made of plaster and glue and spread on a surface to prepare it for painting.

GRAFFITI—words or a drawing, often made without permission, on a public or private surface.

GUM ARABIC—a water-soluble resin that is produced by several kinds of acacia plants. Gum arabic is used in art as a binder.

HIEROGLYPH—a picture that is used to convey a word or sound; ancient Egyptians used hieroglyphic writing.

MEDIUM—the materials used by an artist to create a work of art.

MOSAIC—a decoration made by placing together small, colorful pieces of material, such as stones or glass, to form pictures or patterns.

MURAL—a work of art made on or into a wall or a ceiling.

PICTOGRAM—an ancient or prehistoric drawing or painting made on a rock. Pictograms often recorded events or told stories in picture form.

PIGMENT—a powdered substance mixed with a liquid to add color.

PLASTER—a paste (often of lime, water, and sand) that hardens when dry. Plaster is often used to coat walls and ceilings.

POUNCING—the act of dabbing charcoal or chalk through tiny holes poked through the lines of a paper sketch.

ROCK ART—prehistoric or ancient drawings or paintings made on or into stone.

SCAFFOLDING—a temporary, elevated structure used by workers for construction, repair, and decoration of buildings.

SCUMBLING—a painting technique in which a thin coat of half-dry paint is brushed over a dry paint layer, allowing the color underneath to show through.

STENCIL—an image created when ink or paint is applied inside a cutout design or shape; the paint goes through the hole to create a design on the surface underneath.

TROMPE L'OEIL—any visual illusion that makes a painted image appear three-dimensional; this French term means "fool the eye."

UNDERCOAT—the first layer of paint and the base for the layers that follow; it is often used to establish dark or light values.

WALL PAINTING—a painting made on or into a wall. Murals and frescoes are examples of wall paintings.

WHITEWASH—the act of applying a solution, typically of lime and water, to whiten or cover a surface.

INDEX

A

Abomey palace art, 32–35
acid rain, 4
Acosta, Sofia (La Suerte), 65
acrylic, 49, 64
Adams, John Quincy, 44
Afghanistan, 62–65
Agonglo (king of Dahomey), 35
AIDS awareness, 52
airbrush, 39, 70
Ajjawi, Laila, 65
Akaba (king of Dahomey), 35
Alavi, Kani, 55–57
Albro, Maxine, 40, 41
al-Walīd ibn Yazīd, 23
América Tropical (Siqueiros), 67
The *Amistad*, 42–45
anamorphosis, 60, 70
ancient manuscripts, 21
animation, 68
archaeological sites, 16, 66, 67
    Herculaneum, 14–17, 66
    Mogao Grottoes, 18–21, 67
    Queen Nefertari's tomb, 6–9
    Qusayr 'Amra, 22–25
Argentina, 3–5
art as experience, 12
art media, 1, 70
    acrylic, 49, 64
    chalk, 20, 49, 50–51
    clay, 3, 12, 34
    fresco, 14–17, 27, 38, 40, 66, 70
    gesso, 49, 70
    gum arabic, 12, 70
    mosaics, 25, 70
    plant/mineral pigments, 3, 12, 34, 70
    stencils, 3, 20, 70
    tempera, 8
augmented reality, 68

B

Baca, Judith F., 47, 48, 49
Baldwin, Roger, 44
Banksy, 1
Basquiat, Jean-Michel, 53
bas-reliefs, 34–35, 70

Battle of Tristan against the Dragon, Runkelstein Castle, 27
Behanzin (king of Dahomey), 34–35
Benin, Republic of, 32–35
Berlin Wall, 54–57
Bible, book of Genesis, 30
The Big Three, 37–39
binder, 3, 70
The Birth of Rock and Roll (Baca), 49
blowtorch, 39, 70
blueprints, 48, 70
Brazil, 1, 65
Buddhist art, 19–21, 64, 67

C

California (Albro), 41
carnation pollen, 12
cartoon, 30, 70
Castro, Panmela (Brazil's graffiti queen), 65
cave art, 3–5, 20, 21, 70
Cave of the Hands, 2–5
Centre Dramatique series (Ella and Pitr), 60
chalk, 20, 49, 50
Charles VII (king of Naples), 16
China, 18–21, 67
Chinese Massacre (1871), 48
CHU, 64
clay, 3, 12, 34
Coit, Lillian "Firebelle", 40
Coit Tower murals, 40–41
conservation. *See* mural preservation
"Contemporary Aspects of Life in California," 40
Crack Is Wack (Haring), 50–53
Cuba, 43

D

Dahomey, 32–35
Devi, Sita, 13
Dreaming Graffiti series (Hassani), 64

drug abuse, 52
Durga (Devi), 13

E

East Germany, 55, 56
East Side Gallery (Berlin Wall), 54–57
economic inequality, 40
Ecuador, 65
Edjo, 8
Egypt, 7–9
Egyptian Book of the Dead, 7
El Pueblo de Los Angeles Historical Monument, 67
Ella and Pitr, 58–61
engrave, 5, 70
enslavement, 43–45
Ethnicities (Kobra), 1
European Middle Ages, 26–27

F

Fon people, 32–35
foreshortening, 30, 70
French colonial army, 34
fresco, 14–17, 27, 38, 40, 66, 70

G

Germany, 54–57
The Germen Crew, 1
gesso, 49, 70
Getty Conservation Institute, 8, 66, 67
Glélé (king of Dahomey), 35
Gonzales, David M., 48
graffiti, 50–53, 62–65, 70
Graffiti at Dural Aman (Hassani), 62–63
graffito, 53
grave robbers, 9
Great Depression, 40
The Great Wall of Los Angeles, 46–49
Guezo (king of Dahomey), 34, 35
gum arabic, 12, 70
Gymnast (Banksy), 1

H

hand lettering, 53
handprints, 2–5
Haring, Keith, 50–53
Hassani, Shamsia, 62–65
Heimler, Gabriel, 57
Herculaneum, 14–17, 66
hieroglyph, 6–7, 70
Hinduism, 11–12, 13
The History of California (The Great Wall of Los Angeles), 46–49
The History of Mexico (Rivera), 36–37
Holocaust, 48
Horus, 8
Houegbadja (king of Dahomey), 35

I

illusion, 31, 60
immigrants, 48
India, 10–13
Indigenous peoples, 1, 37, 39, 48, 67
Islam, 23, 65
Italy, 14–17, 26–27, 28
It Happened in November (Alavi), 57

J

Janaka (king of Mithila), 11
Jordan, 22–25, 65

K

kaolin, 3
Keer, Leon, 68
Kinder, Birgit, 56
Kobra, Eduardo, 1
kohbar ghar, 12

L

LGBTQ+ community, 48, 52
Library (Zakheim), 41
Lilith and Olaf (Ella and Pitr),
    58–61
Los Angeles River, 47
Los Tres Grandes (The Big
    Three), 36–39

M

Macro Mural of Palmitas
    (The Germen Crew), 1
The Making of a Fresco
    Showing the Building of a
    City (Rivera), 38
materials. *See* art media
media. *See* art media
Mexico, 1, 36–39
Michelangelo, 28–31, 39
Mithila Kohbar paintings,
    10–13
Mogao Grottoes, 18–21, 67
mosaics, 25, 70
Mount Vesuvius eruption
    (79 CE), 14–17, 66
mural, defined, 1, 70
mural preservation, 66–68
    Abomey palace art, 35
    Cave of the Hands, 4
    Herculaneum, 66
    Mogao Grottoes, 21
    Queen Nefertari's tomb, 8
musical instruments, 64

N

Nefertari (queen of Egypt), 6–9
Nekhbet, 8
New Deal, 40
Nightmare series (Hassani), 64
Nine-Story Temple (Mogao),
    18–19
Norway, 58–61
Nuart street art festival (2015),
    58

O

Olaf I (king of Norway), 61
Orozco, José Clemente, 37, 38
Osiris, 8

P

pictogram, 34, 70
pigments, plant/mineral, 3, 12,
    34, 70
Pleasant, Mary Ellen, 48
pollution, 49, 66
pouncing, 20, 30, 70
Prehistoric California (Baca),
    48
projection mapping, 68
Public Works of Art Project
    (PWAP) (United States),
    40

Q

Queen Nefertari's tomb, 6–9
Qusayr 'Amra, 22–25

R

racial injustice, 45, 53
Rama (prince of Ayodhya), 12
Ramayana, 11
Ramses the Great (pharaoh of
    Egypt), 7
The Repatriation of the Freed
    Captives (Woodruff), 44
Rivera, Diego, 36–40, 45
rock art, 3–5, 70
Roman wall frescoes,
    Herculaneum, 14–17, 66
Roosevelt, Franklin D., 40
Runkelstein Castle, 26–27

S

salt crystals, 8
San Francisco Art Institute,
    38, 39

scaffolding, 48, 70
scumbling, 49, 70
Self-portrait (Orozco), 38
Self-portrait (Siqueiros), 39
senet, 8
Shattering (Keer), 68
Shiva's bow, 11–12
Silk Road, 19, 21
Siqueiros, David Alfaro, 37–39,
    47, 67
Sistine Chapel, 28–31
social realism, 39, 45
Spek, Joost, 68
star maps, 25
stencils, 3, 20, 70
street art, 1, 53, 58, 62–65
symbolism, 4, 25, 35, 50, 56

T

Taliban, 64, 65
Talladega College, 45
tempera paint, 8
termite mounds, 34
Test the Rest (Kinder), 56
tomb paintings, 7–8
Tournament Room,
    Runkelstein Castle, 27
The Trial of the Amistad
    Captives (Woodruff),
    44–45
Tristan and Isolde, 26
trompe l'oeil (fool the eye), 31,
    70

U

Umayyad dynasty, 23–25
undercoat, 49, 70
UNESCO World Heritage site,
    4, 7, 14, 19, 22, 32
United Kingdom, 55, 64
United States, 40–41, 42–45,
    46–49

V

Valley of the Queens (Egypt), 7
vandalism, 4, 21, 66
Vatican City, 28–31
Vintler, Niklaus and Franz,
    26–27

W

The Wall Jumper (Heimler), 57
Wang Yuanlu, 21
weather exposure, 66
West Africa, 43
We the Youth (Haring), 52
whitewash, 65, 67, 70
women artists
    in Dahomey, 34
    empowerment and, 12,
        32–35, 62–65
    exclusion of, 11
    Mithila style and, 10–13
Woodruff, Hale, 44, 45
workers' rights, 39, 40
World War II, 55

Y

Yuezun, 19, 21

Z

Zakheim, Bernard, 40, 41
Zodiac Dome, Qusayr 'Amra, 25